When Your Life Suddenly Stopped

Living After a Suicide Loss

Romina Ericksen

For everyone whose life was changed by suicide in a single moment, and who has had to learn how to keep living with what followed. For my family, and for all those who were there for us in our hardest time — and who are still here.

This book contains material related to suicide, loss, and grief. Some passages may be emotionally intense or distressing.

Table of Contents

Prologue..1

Part I: The Rupture...7

Before Everything Changed..8

Chapter 1 - The News...14

Chapter 2 - The First Hours After...........................22

Chapter 3 – The Place...28

Part II: The Unraveling..36

Chapter 4 – Afterward...37

Chapter 5 – One last Time......................................43

Chapter 6 – The Funeral..50

Chapter 7 – The Puzzle Left Behind.......................58

Chapter 8 – The Question Of Guilt.........................69

Chapter 9 – Silence...76

Part III: The Road Ahead...83

Chapter 10 – What Remains....................................84

Chapter 11 – Going On..92

Chapter 12 – What Stays..102

Chapter 13 – If You Are Here.................................110

1981 - 2024

Prologue

There are moments in life that change everything, not only because of what happens in them, but because from that moment on, nothing is ever experienced in quite the same way again.

They draw an invisible line through a life, a line that separates what came before from everything that follows.

For those who lose someone they love to suicide, that moment is rarely contained within a single second. It is more like a state into which a person is suddenly thrown, a condition in which reality shifts shape and everything that once felt certain begins to lose its balance. You wake in the morning as you would on any other day.

Maybe sunlight is coming through the window, or maybe it is raining. Outside, there may be passing cars, distant voices, or the quiet sounds of people beginning the routines of an ordinary morning.

And yet later, when you look back, this will be the day you remember for the rest of your life.

The day your own life came to a sudden stop.

When someone dies by suicide, what remains is not only absence. What remains is also a space filled with questions, and those questions do not always arrive all at once. Sometimes they force their way into the mind immediately. Sometimes they surface only weeks or months later, when the first shock has quieted just enough for thought to begin moving again.

Why? Should I have noticed something? Could I have prevented it? What did I miss?

These questions can be loud, insistent, and relentless. But they can also settle more quietly, taking root deep within the mind and returning again and again, as though they are still searching for an answer that may never fully come.

Many survivors describe the moment after such a loss as a kind of inner standstill. While everything outside continues moving, while people go to work, buy groceries, laugh, complain, make plans, and carry on with the ordinary business of being alive, their own life suddenly feels as though time has stopped. It can feel as though they themselves have been left standing still while the rest of the world keeps turning without interruption.

Losing someone to suicide is a particular kind of grief. Not because the pain is somehow greater than other forms of loss, since pain cannot be measured that way, but because it is so often accompanied by things many survivors carry for a very long time: guilt, doubt, shock, and a deep, almost unrelenting need to understand what may never be fully understandable.

And yet understanding often remains out of reach.

Memories begin to change under the pressure of that loss. Conversations that once seemed ordinary no longer feel ordinary. A glance, a sentence, a single moment from the past can suddenly appear charged with meaning, as though something hidden might be waiting there to be discovered. The mind begins trying to make sense of what happened by working backward, fitting memories together like pieces of a puzzle, looking for patterns, connections, and causes, anything that might make the whole picture hold.

But many of those pieces do not form a clear answer.

And that can be one of the hardest things to bear.

As human beings, we are shaped by the desire to understand. We look for reasons, for coherence, for some thread that can lead us through confusion and bring us to a place that makes sense. We want to know how something happened, why it happened, and whether anything could have changed it. But after a suicide, many of those answers remain in darkness, and no amount of searching can guarantee that they will come into view.

What remains instead is a path, a path no one would ever choose, no one would willingly step onto, and no one is ever truly prepared to walk. And yet many people do walk it. They walk it quietly, often without language for what they are carrying, often unseen by those around them, and sometimes with the overwhelming feeling of being completely alone in what they have been left to live with.

But they are not alone.

This book grew out of my own experience. It is not a clinical explanation of grief, and it does not offer simple answers, because simple answers do not exist for a loss like this. What it offers instead is an honest attempt to look directly at what remains when someone dies by suicide. It is a book about loss, about unanswered questions, about guilt, about memory, and about the difficult and often contradictory reality of continuing to live after something that changes everything.

You may recognize yourself in some of these thoughts. There may be passages in which you feel understood in ways you have not often felt understood before. Or your own experience may have unfolded differently, in ways these pages cannot fully name. That too is part of grief.

It does not move in a straight line, and it does not follow a fixed pattern. It does not disappear simply because time passes. It changes. At times it grows quieter. At others it returns without warning, as immediate as ever.

A song on the radio, a scent, a place, a sentence, a time of year. Any of these can be enough to bring everything back in an instant. Many people believe grief must eventually be over, as though it were something one leaves behind completely. But for many survivors, that is not how it feels. The loss becomes part of the structure of their life.

It remains a chapter in their story, not always at the center, not always equally loud, but never entirely gone.

This book hopes to show that it is possible to live with that chapter, even if it never fully disappears. Not by solving it, and not by leaving it behind, but by learning, slowly and imperfectly, how to carry what remains.

This book may be a small companion on that path, a companion through memory, through difficult days, through questions that do not fully resolve, and through those quieter moments in which life, almost without asking permission, begins to move again.

Because even when life feels as though it has come to a complete stop, movement does return. Not all at once. Not loudly. But slowly, quietly, and often almost imperceptibly, until one day it becomes clear that something, however small, has begun again.

And that is where the journey this book tells begins.

Part I: The Rupture

Before Everything Changed

When I look back now at the time before his death, it no longer appears to me as one single moment that suddenly changed everything. What I remember instead is a series of small, almost imperceptible shifts, moments that barely stood out at the time and simply moved past in the current of everyday life. Only later, after everything had already happened, did they begin to take on a different meaning in my memory.

In the beginning, our life was the way one hopes it will be at the start of a relationship. We shared our routines, our thoughts, and our stories.

After work, we often sat together, sometimes at the kitchen table, sometimes on the couch, and told each other whatever the day had brought with it. Those conversations were nothing extraordinary, and yet they were exactly what created our closeness. They could last for an hour or two without either of us noticing how quickly time was passing.

There was an easy familiarity between us, a quiet sense that we could tell each other anything.

When our daughter was born, our daily life changed, of course. The nights became shorter, sleep more restless, and suddenly everything revolved around this small new life that had expanded our world in such a beautiful way. In those first months, all of it seemed normal to me. So many parents pass through that season of exhaustion and adjustment. You grow used to a new rhythm, and little by little you find your way through days and nights that no longer follow the structure they once had.

But a few months after she was born, something began to change, at first so subtly that it was difficult to grasp. He came home from work more and more exhausted, not merely tired, but as if each day had taken a little more out of him than the day before. Of course, I could see that he was happy about us, about our daughter, and about the home we had built together. And yet there was something there that I could not quite reach.

His energy seemed to run out more quickly than it once had, as though every new day demanded more from him than the last.

I remember many evenings from that period, and the pattern was almost always the same. At some point, our little daughter would fall asleep, the house would grow quiet, and the part of the day that had once belonged to us should have begun. Before that, we would have sat down together, perhaps eaten something, or simply talked about the day, about small worries, and about whatever thoughts had followed us into the evening.

Yet little by little, that very moment began to change.

He sat beside me, and more and more often I had the feeling that inwardly he was somewhere far away. If I asked him something, he answered, but often only after a pause, as though he first had to search for the words. So much remained on the surface. We had once spoken about everything without needing to think about it. Now I sometimes had the impression that every additional word required effort from him.

The closeness between us changed as well, not abruptly and not because of one great argument or one clearly defined event, but quietly, almost invisibly. He sought it out less than before.

It was not a deliberate withdrawal, nor an obvious distance that could easily be named.

It was more like a slow drifting apart, the kind that hardly registers at first because daily life keeps moving and because so much of what changes in a relationship changes in silence. And yet there came a moment when I realized that something had shifted. I was sitting beside him and suddenly felt something I had never known before: the feeling of no longer truly being seen.

At the time, I could not have explained exactly what had changed. I only knew that something felt different. Sometimes he seemed more irritable than before, as if his patience had grown shorter. Small things we once might have laughed about now seemed to unsettle him much more quickly.

I often told myself that perhaps it was simply the strain of everyday life, too little sleep, too many demands pressing in on us all at once, and too much responsibility arriving at the same time.

When I look back now, what I remember most clearly is his expression. At the time, I did not consciously notice it, but later I began to see it again in so many photographs. The smile that had once come so naturally appeared less often, and in its place there was sometimes something else in his eyes, something heavy that I did not know how to read then.

It was not a clearly recognizable sadness, nor was it anger. It was more like emptiness, a gaze that seemed to go somewhere without truly seeing anything. Back then, I thought he was simply tired, perhaps overwhelmed by work, perhaps worn down by the nights when our daughter kept both of us awake.

There were so many plausible explanations that I did not look beyond them. Life kept going. Days passed. Weeks passed. From the outside, everything seemed to continue as it always had. And yet beneath that surface, something had already begun to change, something I could neither name nor fully understand at the time.

Only much later did I realize that something fundamental had already started to shift during that period, quietly, almost unnoticed, and yet with a force that would eventually leave a permanent mark on our lives. Back then, it was only a feeling, a vague kind of knowing somewhere in the background of my mind, something I could not yet make sense of.

Life continued, the way it always does, and I never would have imagined that everything was about to change so soon.

Chapter 1 - The News

For me, that day began like any other ordinary day, one of those days that, at first glance, seems no different from the countless others out of which a life is made. Nothing in those early hours suggested that this would later become one of the most devastating days of my entire life. I moved through familiar routines, through the small, habitual patterns that give shape to an ordinary day, carrying out the kinds of tasks that repeat themselves so often that one usually never pauses to think about them at all.

Only much later did I begin to understand that the story of that day had not really begun that morning.

Looking back, I can see that an invisible trail led far into the months and years before it. Especially during the last two years, I had increasingly felt that something in him was changing. At first, these changes had been small and difficult to define, more a shift in atmosphere than anything that could be clearly named. Conversations that had once felt natural and effortless became shorter. Thoughts he once might have spoken aloud remained unspoken. Sometimes we sat beside each other in the same room, and yet I had the distinct feeling that a quiet distance had begun to grow between us.

It was not a sudden change, nor one dramatic enough to make itself immediately visible. It was more like a silent shift that worked its way into our daily life slowly and almost unnoticed, until it had become part of the emotional landscape of our days. Today, I can see that this period was already shaped by things I did not fully understand at the time. Every person carries a history inside them, memories, experiences, losses, and wounds that leave their traces behind. Some of those things can be spoken about and shared. Others remain hidden deep within. I knew that he had lived through difficult things, but back then I had no clear sense of how heavily those experiences were still weighing on him.

At that time, I still believed that time could heal most things. Today, I know that some wounds simply grow quieter without ever fully disappearing.

But that morning, I knew none of this yet.

Around midday, I picked up my older daughter from school and then my younger one from her playgroup. Everything unfolded exactly as it had on so many other days before. We drove the familiar roads, exchanged a few words with other parents, and moved through the small routines and gestures that make up an ordinary family day. Looking back, it is precisely these unremarkable moments that now appear with such painful clarity in my memory, perhaps because they belonged to the last hours in which life still seemed completely normal.

In the early afternoon, the mail carrier rang the bell and handed me a small package. When I glanced at the sender, my eyes lingered there for a moment. I was surprised, because I had not expected him to send me anything. For an instant, I wondered what might be inside, but the thought was fleeting and was quickly absorbed again into the ordinary flow of the afternoon.

I carried the package into the house and placed it on the table for the moment. My older daughter noticed it immediately. Children have an astonishing sensitivity to anything new or slightly out of place, and the moment the package appeared, her curiosity awakened. She wanted to know what was inside and whether we could open it right away. I told her that I did not know yet either, and that we could look inside together a little later.

At that moment, I still assumed it might be some small surprise, or perhaps simply something ordinary. But first I had to take care of lunch, because the little one was hungry. So I set the package aside and began preparing the meal. The next half hour passed without anything remarkable happening. I moved around the kitchen, made lunch, spoke with the children, and carried out the many small tasks that make up an ordinary afternoon.

And yet, while I was doing all of this, my older daughter never quite lost sight of that package. Again and again she asked whether we could finally open it, and eventually I sat down with her at the dining table, took the package into my hands, and began opening it slowly.

At that point, I had no idea that within the next few minutes my life was about to change completely.

When I opened the package, I first saw several personal belongings. They were things that had clearly been chosen deliberately, keepsakes, objects carrying meaning. Among them was a letter. It had been printed out and was obviously written on a computer. While my older daughter sat beside me, listening closely, I began reading it aloud. After lunch, I had laid the little one down for a nap, and she was now asleep on the couch in the living room, peaceful and completely unaware.

The letter was long, and as I read it, a feeling began slowly to rise inside me, though at first I could not fully name it. Something about the words felt different from ordinary writing. The sentences sounded unfamiliar, and at the same time they carried a strange sense of finality. About halfway through, I stopped for a moment and turned to my older daughter.

Quietly, I told her that all of this felt strange somehow, almost as though I were reading a farewell letter.

And yet I kept reading.

Then, suddenly, she noticed that there was another note in the package. I reached for it. This note was handwritten. While the first letter had been typed on a computer, only a few lines appeared on this page.

It said that I should notify the police. It also contained instructions about where certain things could be found, where the keys were, and where the car was parked.

At the end were words that burned themselves into my memory forever.

He was sorry. I should please forgive him.

As I read those lines, something inside me collapsed. Tears ran down my face, and I began to scream, because my mind refused to understand what those words could possibly mean. I grabbed the phone and called the police. With a trembling voice, I tried to explain what I had just read and what had been inside that package.

The voice on the other end of the line remained calm and matter-of-fact. I was told to stay where I was and that someone would contact me.

Then began a period of waiting that, looking back, can hardly be measured in minutes or hours.

It lasted around two hours, but in my experience it stretched into an endless chain of suspended moments. I walked through the house again and again without really knowing what I was doing. I would sit down, then stand up again, go to the front door, return to the living room, and keep looking at my phone as though it might somehow break the reality of what was happening.

All the while, my mind searched desperately for an explanation less final than the words on that note. Maybe I had misunderstood everything. Maybe there was some other way to explain the situation. But at the same time, a fear was growing inside me that could no longer be pushed aside. Meanwhile, my daughter occupied herself in the living room as though everything were normal, and yet even in her one could see the uncertainty of the moment. That image, of something outwardly still looking so ordinary while, inside me, an entire world was beginning to come apart, has remained deeply etched in my memory.

When the doorbell finally rang, I already knew that this moment would mark a boundary beyond which nothing would ever be the same.

Two female police officers stood at the door.

They explained calmly that they needed to speak with me. As they entered the room, I went almost automatically into the kitchen, picked up a cleaning cloth, and began wiping down the counter, even though it was already clean. It was as though my body was trying to hold on to something familiar and repetitive while everything inside me resisted what was about to be spoken aloud.

One of the officers eventually asked whether I was Romina Ericksen. At first, I did not respond, because although I heard the question, I could not truly allow it to reach me. Only after she addressed me again, gently and calmly, did I finally sit down at the table. And when I looked into their faces, I already knew what they were about to say.

The words that followed merely confirmed what, in that moment, I had already understood:

my husband had not been found alive.

In that instant, everything inside me broke open. I kept repeating that it could not be true, that it could not be right. At the same time, I pointed toward the couch in the living room, where my two-and-a-half-year-old daughter was sleeping peacefully, as though the world were still entirely in order. And while cars passed outside and people continued on with their ordinary lives, I realized with devastating clarity that my own life had changed irrevocably.

Nothing would ever be the same again.

Chapter 2 - The First Hours After

When the two police officers finally left the house and the front door closed behind them, a silence remained that is almost impossible to describe, though even now I can still feel the weight of it.

It was not the ordinary kind of silence that follows when visitors leave or when a conversation has simply come to an end. This silence seemed to possess a substance of its own, as though the air itself had changed and settled differently over everything around me. It lay over the rooms, over the furniture, and over me, as if the whole house were holding its breath.

By then, the emergency pastoral counselor had already arrived. She sat down beside me, spoke in a calm and steady voice, and tried to offer some kind of support. I heard her words and saw her lips moving, but nothing she said truly reached me. Her voice existed in the room, and yet it seemed to stop somewhere in front of me, as though it had touched an invisible barrier and could go no further. Everything felt wrapped in a kind of fog.

It was as if I were standing outside myself, watching the world continue to move while I remained separated from it by something I could not cross. People were speaking to one another. Footsteps moved through the house. Doors opened and closed. And somewhere in the middle of all of it, I sat there with the strange and frightening feeling that my own body no longer fully belonged to me.

Those first minutes after the news remain, even now, like a brief blackout in my memory. Maybe it was ten minutes. Maybe half an hour. I still cannot say with certainty. Time lost all clear structure in that moment. Individual seconds seemed to stretch endlessly, while entire sections of memory blurred into something shapeless and indistinct. What I do remember is hearing words without understanding them. My mind felt empty, as though it had gone blank in self-defense.

My body felt drained, as if all strength had been pulled out of it in a matter of moments. And within me there was only a single thought, repeated with an almost desperate simplicity:

I wanted to sleep. I did not want to hear anything anymore, or think anything, or feel anything. More than anything, I wanted to disappear from that reality, if only for a moment. At some point, I lay down to rest, while someone else took care of the children. Even now, I cannot clearly remember who helped me or how I actually got to the bedroom. Everything seemed to happen automatically, as though my body was carrying out movements my mind could barely follow. In order to calm down at all, I took anti-anxiety medication and sleeping pills that I still had at home.

It was not an attempt to escape so much as a desperate effort to give my body a brief pause, just enough to make it possible for me to get through the night and still somehow be there for my children the next day. When I finally fell asleep, the sleep was anything but restful. The images from that day were still too fresh, too raw, too impossible to comprehend. I dreamed of him, and then suddenly I jolted awake, shooting upright in bed and instinctively grabbing at my throat as I fought for air. For a moment, I was convinced that I was suffocating. My heart was beating so violently that I could feel it pounding in my throat. Only after several seconds did the world slowly begin to come back into focus.

I recognized the room, the bed, the familiar furniture around me. I understood where I was. I understood that I was alive, that I could breathe, and that my children were still in the house. And yet everything around me still felt utterly unreal, as though none of it quite belonged to the same world. Those first hours after the news still blur together in my memory. Much of it feels as though someone laid a veil over it, softening certain details while leaving others with unbearable sharpness. In the days that followed, my body began reacting in ways I had never experienced before. For four days, I could not eat. Every time I tried to take even the smallest bite, nausea rose in me immediately. Even the thought of food made my stomach revolt.

Drinking was difficult too. I could barely manage more than half a glass of water, or occasionally two small glasses of wine in the evening.

It felt as though my body had switched into some kind of shock state, abandoning all ordinary rhythms of hunger, thirst, and rest. But outside of me, the world did not stop. The very next day, reality began forcing its way back in. The criminal investigation unit called, and shortly afterward the funeral home did too. Conversations had to be held. Questions had to be answered.

Decisions had to be made, and not just any decisions, but decisions about things no one ever wants to think about, let alone decide in the immediate aftermath of such a loss. Each one of those phone calls pulled me a little further back into a reality that, inwardly, I still could not fully grasp.

The mornings were especially hard. Every time I woke up, there was that one brief moment, that tiny suspended instant in which my mind had not yet remembered what had happened. In that moment, everything still felt normal, and for a few seconds I could believe that maybe it had all only been a nightmare. But the thought never lasted long. Within seconds the memory returned, and with it came that cold, merciless certainty: it had not been a nightmare. It was reality. And yet through all the fog in my mind, one thought kept breaking through again and again: my children. Everything else could wait. Everything else was secondary. In those first hours and days, the only thing that truly mattered was somehow finding enough strength to be there for them.

I also spoke briefly with his mother. The police had arranged for officers to go to his parents' home at the same time the two officers were with me, and that was how we were informed at the same time. We spoke on the phone afterward.

She sounded calm, at least outwardly, but of course she was in shock as well.

She had already lost one son to suicide before, and now she was being forced to endure that pain a second time. That fact alone was almost impossible to comprehend. At that point, my own parents still knew nothing. At some point that day, my mother sent me a message asking, "Is everything okay? We haven't heard from you at all today." I answered only briefly: "Mom, I can't talk right now. I'll get back to you later. Don't worry, I'm okay." Later, my parents told me that the moment they read that message, they knew something was wrong. The tone had been different from usual. And yet, even then, they wanted to give me space until I was able to reach out to them myself. It was not until late that evening that I finally spoke with them on the phone.

By the next day, they were already on their way to me.

Chapter 3 – The Place

When I held the key in my hand that morning, I knew that I was about to open a door behind which nothing would ever be the same again.

The key felt heavy, not because of its actual weight, but because of what it had suddenly come to represent. Behind that door was a place that only a few days earlier had still belonged to the ordinary fabric of everyday life, a place we had entered and left without giving it any particular thought. And yet that very place had now become something else entirely. It had become a threshold, a dividing line between the life I had lived up to that moment and the life that was now waiting ahead of me.

There are places that remain unremarkable for an entire lifetime, places where nothing seems to happen except the ordinary business of daily life. You come and go, set things down, take care of small practical tasks, and never imagine that one day this exact place might take on a meaning so different from everything it once held.

And yet sometimes that is exactly what happens. You return, and suddenly everything has changed. The walls are still standing where they always stood, the furniture has not moved, and nothing visible seems out of place. The entire place feels altered, as though something invisible has shifted and can never be shifted back again.

The day before, the door had already been opened by the police. The keys had not been found where he had said they would be in his farewell letter, and so a locksmith had eventually been called. After the officers entered the house, everything was locked again, and a criminal investigation seal was placed over the lock, a visible sign that behind this door, something had happened that could never be undone. The next day, I was allowed to pick up the keys from the police station, and that meant it was now up to me to go there and break that seal myself. I never could have done that alone.

When my father found out, he reacted immediately. Without hesitation, he said in a calm, steady voice that I would not be going there by myself. "You're not going there alone," he said.

"I'm coming with you." My father had once been a police officer, and in the course of his work he had seen places where people were confronted with situations they never could have imagined beforehand. He knew what can be waiting behind a door when something terrible has happened.

But this time was different. This was not some call-out involving strangers. This time, it was about his son-in-law, and it was about his daughter. Together, we drove to the police station to pick up the key. I barely remember the conversation there. Everything felt muted, as though I were moving through some thick gray layer that dulled everything around me. Voices sounded distant. Questions were asked, and I answered them automatically, without truly taking in what was being said.

In the meantime, my mother stayed with the children. Then came the moment I had been dreading the entire time. We left the police station, walked silently to the car, and set off.

Hardly anyone spoke during the drive. The landscape passed by outside the window, fields, houses, roads, but I barely registered any of it. My eyes were turned outward, but nothing I saw truly reached me. Again and again, the same question returned to my mind: what would be waiting for me there?

When we finally pulled into the driveway, we parked the car and got out. For a moment, I simply stood there. Even the air felt heavy, as though it were no longer moving properly. Together, we crossed the yard slowly and made our way toward the house. The front door was farther back, around the corner, and the moment we turned that corner and approached it, I saw it immediately: the police seal. The sticker from the criminal investigation unit had been placed directly over the lock, covering the point where the key would need to go in. It had been positioned in such a way that the door could not be opened without breaking it.

In that moment, that small sticker carried an enormous weight. It made visible what had happened behind that door, and it gave form to a truth no one would ever wish to face. It felt like a boundary in the most literal sense. On this side of the door, there was still some remnant of my old life. On the other side, reality was waiting.

My father went to the door first. With calm, controlled movements, he removed the seal. For a brief moment, he paused, as though even he needed to gather himself one last time before crossing that threshold. Then he turned to me and said quietly, "You stay here. I'm going in first."

I nodded. The seconds while he was inside the house felt endless. Standing outside the door, I felt a fear that was so deep it seemed almost physical. My heart was beating faster, and every passing second stretched out as though time itself were slowing down. Then the door opened again. My father stood in the doorway and said, with the same calm steadiness, "You can come in." Slowly, I stepped inside.

The room was still in a way that felt unnatural. It was not an ordinary stillness, but a silence so heavy that it seemed to have settled into the walls, the floor, and the furniture themselves. Directly across from me hung pictures of us on the wall, photographs of me and the children. He had put them there. They were the last things he wanted to see before leaving this world. The moment my eyes fell on them, something inside me gave way. On the floor lay a small earring, and when I saw it, my legs suddenly failed me and I sank down right there.

On the kitchen counter were his things: his ID, his keys, and a few personal belongings.

Everything had been laid out neatly beside one another, not carelessly, but deliberately, almost with care. It looked as though he had taken a moment to hold those things in his hands one final time before placing them there. Next to them stood six empty beer bottles. The dishwasher had already finished running. He had also washed and dried laundry beforehand, and in the bedroom there were still clean clothes lying there, though they had not yet been folded. It looked as though something had stopped in the middle of ordinary life. As though a life had come to a sudden standstill.

My father opened the windows to let fresh air into the house, but the heaviness of that place could not be driven out so easily. At some point, my eyes fell on the patio door. Almost without thinking, I walked slowly toward it until I was standing directly in front of it.

Without even realizing I was doing it, I placed my hand against the glass. It felt cool beneath my palm. And in that exact moment, a memory came back. About a year earlier, he had stood in that very same spot, looking out into the backyard for a long time without saying anything. At first, I had not thought much of it.

But the longer he remained there, the more strongly I felt that something was going on inside him, something he was not putting into words. Finally, I had said, “Hey, what’s wrong?” At first, he did not answer.

Only after several seconds did he say, in a calm voice, that he did not want to talk about it right then. But I did not let it go.

After a while, he finally began to speak. His voice was calm, almost matter-of-fact, when he said that in his life he had never really finished anything. Then he paused. “But I still have one ace up my sleeve,” he said. At the time, I had no idea what he meant. When I asked what he was referring to, he only shook his head slightly and said, “You don’t need to understand that now. There’s still time.” Then he looked at me once more and added, “But I promise you this: when the time comes, you’ll be the first to know.”

Back then, those words had sounded puzzling, almost impossible to place. Today, I know how serious he meant them. Slowly, the memory faded again, and I found myself once more standing there with my hand against the glass of the patio door. At some point, I realized that we had to leave. Part of me did not want to leave that place, as though walking away from it would mean losing something for good. And yet at the same time, I knew I could not remain there.

When I finally turned and looked back one last time, I had the unmistakable feeling that this place would remain part of my life forever.

There are places one eventually leaves behind. And then there are places one walks away from without ever truly leaving, because some part of oneself remains there forever.

Part II: The Unraveling

Chapter 4 – Afterward

A period began that, even now, is difficult to place into any clear sequence of events. When I look back on the days after the news, what I remember is not a clear line of one day following the next, but a stretch of time blurred at the edges, marked by deep exhaustion, inward overwhelm, and a feeling so difficult to name that even now it resists being fully put into words. While the world around me seemed to continue as though nothing had happened, it felt to me as though my own time had suddenly stopped, as though everything essential within me had been suspended. Outside, life continued in its familiar rhythm.

People went to work. Children played in the streets. Cars moved through town as they always had, and the days themselves seemed to proceed according to a logic that had not been interrupted. But inside me, nothing moved in the same way. It felt as though someone had taken hold of time itself and stopped it, leaving me in a state that was neither fully past nor fully present, neither able to return to what had been nor yet able to enter what would come next. At first, we shared the news only within the family. Even so, it spread more quickly than I expected. Coworkers reached out, as did friends, acquaintances, and people from different parts of our lives. At his workplace, too, the news caused deep shock. Many could not comprehend what had happened, and again and again the same questions surfaced, whether they were spoken gently or directly.

At their core, they were always the same: How could this have happened? Why had no one noticed anything? He was still so young. Why had he chosen this path? They were the same questions that kept returning in my own mind, and yet I had no answers for them either.

And while all of these conversations, messages, and reactions pressed in on me from the outside, another phase began at the same time: suddenly there were countless practical matters that had to be handled, matters for which no one ever prepares you. There were conversations with the funeral director, decisions about the funeral itself, about where the service would be held, and about countless details no one imagines having to think through in the middle of such a collapse.

So many of those questions felt deeply wrong to me, as though they did not belong to the reality I was living in. While one part of my life had completely fallen apart, the world was suddenly expecting decisions, paperwork, logistics, and practical arrangements. Documents had to be filled out. Phone calls had to be made. Appointments had to be coordinated. It felt as though an entire wave of bureaucracy had collided with a moment in which I was barely capable of holding a clear thought in place.

There were times when I sat staring at a sheet of paper for what felt like an eternity without truly understanding what was written there. My mind was trying to function, trying to make decisions and move things forward, while inside me everything felt emptied out and far away. At times, I even had the strange sensation of observing myself from a distance, as though I were carrying on conversations, making arrangements, and signing documents while another part of me had gone almost entirely silent and barely seemed to move at all.

Alongside all of this, a growing need to withdraw began to take hold in me. The thought of encountering other people often felt unbearable.

It was as though every glance and every encounter would instantly expose what had happened, as though the fact of my loss had become something visible that I could not hide even if I wanted to. Because of that, many things were taken over by others. Family and friends went grocery shopping, brought food, and took care of small errands. Things that normally seem so ordinary and self-evident suddenly became obstacles I could barely manage on my own. It was not until about two and a half weeks later that I went grocery shopping by myself for the first time, and I still remember that moment with painful clarity.

Even on the way to the store, I could feel how heavy every single step was. It felt as though I were crossing an invisible threshold, one that divided the world in which life had resumed its usual course from the inner reality I was still living in, where nothing had settled and nothing had become normal again.

The grocery store itself had not changed. The shelves stood where they always had. People moved their carts through the aisles, talked to one another, reached for products, and went about their shopping as though it were just another ordinary day.

For everyone else, it was exactly the same place it had been on countless other days. But for me, nothing about it felt ordinary anymore. As I moved slowly through the aisles, I began noticing things I would never have paid attention to before. And then, in the middle of that ordinary store, tears suddenly began running down my face.

Everywhere I looked were things we had once bought together: his favorite bread, the yogurts he especially liked, the beer he sometimes brought home. They were such small, everyday things, the kinds of details no one thinks much about while life is still intact, and yet in that moment they took on a meaning that overwhelmed me completely.

All at once, it became painfully clear that none of those ordinary moments would ever happen for him again. He would never walk through a grocery store again, never stand in front of a shelf deciding what he wanted, never choose a loaf of bread, never take a bottle of beer from the cooler. Those simple routines of daily life had disappeared for good, and it was that finality that struck me there, in the middle of those aisles, with a force no one could ever have prepared me for.

Standing there, I realized something I never could have imagined before: even an entirely ordinary moment, something as simple as a trip to the grocery store, can become the moment in which you feel with devastating clarity how profoundly your life has changed, not because some dramatic outward event was taking place in that instant, but because even the smallest things, the ones once taken for granted, are no longer simple at all.

Chapter 5 – One last Time

At some point, a wish began to grow inside me, one that at first announced itself only quietly. In the beginning, it was little more than a passing thought, something that rose for a brief moment and then disappeared again before I could fully hold onto it. But as the days went on, it returned more and more often, until it no longer felt like a passing thought at all, but like something steady, insistent, and impossible to push away.

I wanted to see him one more time.

At that point, I still could not truly grasp what had happened. My mind understood, at least on the level of facts, that he was dead, but my heart refused to accept that reality completely. Everything still felt unreal, as though I were moving in a space between knowing and refusing to believe, between what had already happened and what some part of me still could not allow to become fully real.

One part of me knew that he was not coming back. That part understood that his life had ended and that nothing could undo that fact. And yet, at the same time, there was another part in me, quiet, desperate, and unwilling to surrender, that still resisted this reality. It kept whispering the same thought to me over and over again: if I could just see him one more time, then perhaps I would finally understand what had happened. Perhaps something inside me would begin to accept what my mind already knew.

The feeling grew stronger with each passing day, until I was convinced that I needed to see him with my own eyes one last time. Only then, I believed, would something inside me begin to understand that what had happened had truly become real. Without that moment, I felt I would remain trapped in a state of suspension, unable to comprehend fully what I had lost.

So I spoke to the funeral director about this wish. I tried to explain to him how important this step felt to me and how deeply I believed that, without it, I would never truly understand what had happened. Even now, I am grateful that no one placed obstacles in my way. I was not met with resistance, discomfort, or distance, but with understanding, patience, and a quiet steadiness that made it possible for me to take that difficult step at all.

On the second day after the news, I went there for the first time. When I arrived, the funeral director did not let me go in right away. Instead, we remained outside for a while and spoke. In calm, careful words, he explained what I should expect and tried to prepare me, gently and respectfully, for what that moment would be like.

I could sense that he was trying to ease some of my fear, not through many words or dramatic explanations, but through the quiet reassurance of his presence. That calm gradually carried over to me and made it possible for me to move, inwardly as well as outwardly, toward what was waiting behind that door.

At some point, he finally opened the door, and I stepped inside slowly.

The room felt still, unbelievably still. It was a silence that seemed to rest heavily in the room, a silence unlike any I had known before. Nothing moved. No sound could be heard. The stillness was so absolute that it seemed to exist not only around me, but inside me as well.

When I saw him lying there for the first time, the moment felt strange in a way that is difficult to describe. He lay there motionless, and his face looked peaceful, almost as if he were simply asleep. And in that exact instant, an image flashed through my mind with startling clarity. I saw him alive. I saw the warm smile on his face the first time he held our daughter in his arms.

I remembered how carefully he had held her then, almost as if he were afraid of hurting her. At the same time, there had been such unmistakable pride in his eyes, as though he could hardly believe that this tiny little person now belonged to us. That memory came back with such force that it felt, for a moment, as if it were unfolding before me all over again. And then other images followed, not in any clear order, but like fragments of memory rising suddenly and unbidden to the surface, shared laughter, conversations that had stretched late into the night, ordinary moments whose meaning only becomes visible once they are gone forever.

It was those quiet, unremarkable moments of daily life, the ones you barely notice while you are living them, that now returned to me with a particular sharpness. Maybe it was because he lay there looking so peaceful, almost as if he were simply sleeping, and because the contrast between that stillness and the life I remembered was almost unbearable.

Over the next several days, I went back there four days in a row. Each day, I returned because I felt the need to be near him and to remain in that final nearness a little longer. It was as though I were trying, step by step, to understand what had happened, while at the same time holding on to every remaining minute of being near him. There were moments when I simply stood beside him. There were others when I sat down and stayed there in silence. And often, I did nothing but look at his face, as if by doing so I might somehow preserve something that was already slipping beyond reach.

At one point, I took his hand in mine.

The cold I felt then was a cold unlike anything else. It was not merely cool, the way cold skin usually is. It carried something final within it, something absolute and unchangeable, something that made me understand in a way beyond words that the person I was touching would not return. And yet his face still looked as though he had simply lain down for a moment to rest and closed his eyes.

Often, I stood beside him for a long time, looking at him and trying to understand what had happened. No one rushed me. No one pressured me to leave. I was given space, and that space became, in its own quiet way, a final time with him. Sometimes I even spoke to him out loud. Once, I said, "Get up. That's enough now." Another time, I said, "We have a daughter. You have to get up."

Of course, deep inside, I knew he would not get up. One part of me had already understood that reality. But there was still that other part in me, that small, desperate remnant of hope, that continued to resist fully accepting what was real. That part kept whispering that perhaps something might still happen, that perhaps he would move, or perhaps open his eyes. But nothing happened.

The days passed, and eventually the fourth day came. The following day, he was to be transferred to the crematory. As I stood beside him, I knew that this would be the last moment in which I would ever see him like this.

I remained there for a long time, as though every second were trying to press itself deeply into my memory. I looked at his face, his hands, the familiar lines of his features that I knew so well, and I understood that I had to hold this image inside me. Tears ran down my face, and at some point I realized that it was time to leave.

I looked at him one last time, and in that moment it became clear to me that if I walked through that door now, there would be no going back. I would never see him like this again, never again his features, never again his hands, never again this human form before me.

So I walked away slowly, step by step, and when the door closed behind me, I knew that this had been the final goodbye, the goodbye to his physical form, forever.

Chapter 6 – The Funeral

The day of the funeral arrived sooner than I felt inwardly prepared for it. Although roughly two weeks had passed between the news of his death and that day, the time in between had not unfolded in any way that felt normal or measurable. Everything seemed to be happening too quickly and yet, at the same time, with such complete unreality that I often felt as though I were watching events take place from somewhere just outside myself.

Time had taken on a strange rhythm in those days. On the one hand, the hours passed with a pressure that hardly left room to breathe, because there was always something new that needed to be decided, arranged, or answered. On the other hand, certain moments stretched out with such heaviness that it was as though time itself were resisting what was happening, as though it could delay the reality of it by only a few seconds more.

Even before the day itself, one question kept returning to me and stealing sleep from the nights: whether the funeral should be public or take place only within the closest circle of family. It was not a simple practical decision, even if from the outside it may have looked like one. I knew that many people had known him. He had friends, coworkers, and acquaintances, people who might also have felt the need to say goodbye, to stand there one last time and acknowledge that a life had ended. And yet, at the same time, I myself felt barely capable of living through that day in front of many people. The thought of standing before a larger group while my own life had only just collapsed beneath me was more than I could bear.

It was not only the situation itself that frightened me. It was also the feeling that, in that moment, I would not have had the strength to withstand the eyes of others, or the weight of their presence, or the effort of remaining outwardly upright while so much inside me was still broken open. There was chaos in me, grief, shock, disbelief, exhaustion, and even the smallest decisions already felt larger than I could carry. In the end, partly out of respect for his parents' wishes, I decided that the funeral would take place only within the closest family circle.

That decision was not made against anyone else. It was simply the only way I could imagine surviving the day at all.

Emotionally, we would not have been able to bear this goodbye in a larger setting. That was why no public announcement was made beforehand about when or where the funeral would take place.

Only a few days later did the obituary appear in the newspaper and online, stating that the funeral had already taken place within the closest family circle. In conversations afterward, I apologized to some people. I told them that the decision had not been easy for me and that I was sorry if they had not been given the chance to be there and say goodbye with us. And yet I knew there had been no version of that choice that would have felt right to everyone.

If I had allowed some to come, others might have wondered why they had not been included. In the end, this was the only way.

On the day of the funeral, my older daughter was with me, while my younger daughter spent the morning at her playgroup. We had arranged that beforehand with the caregivers because she was still very small at the time, and none of us truly had the emotional capacity to care for her there as well. At the same time, we were trying to create enough space to say goodbye ourselves in a situation that already felt unbearable enough as it was.

When we finally gathered outside the chapel, the funeral director and several family members were already there. The atmosphere was quiet, but not empty. It was filled with that heavy, almost physical stillness that settles over people who have gathered for something they still cannot fully comprehend. We greeted one another softly, embraced, and held on a little longer than we normally would, as though those embraces might offer at least some small steadiness in a moment in which nothing felt steady at all. Some wept openly. Others stood in silence, as if even language had withdrawn in the face of what had happened.

It was a warm day in August. The sun stood high in the sky and cast a bright, almost peaceful light across the cemetery. Birds could be heard in the trees, and a light breeze moved through the leaves. It was one of those summer days on which the world appears untouched, and it was precisely that normality that made the whole thing feel almost impossible to bear. While life outside continued in its familiar way, my own inner world still felt motionless, as though it had not yet understood that time had already moved on.

Inside the chapel, everything had been prepared with dignity. At the front stood the urn, surrounded by flowers, and beside it was a photograph of him wearing that familiar smile I knew so well. The moment my eyes fell on that photograph, I felt something tighten sharply inside my chest, because that smile, so alive, so recognizable, had become a memory, even though part of me still felt as though he ought to walk through the door at any moment.

The funeral director gave a eulogy that was calm and respectful, providing a frame for this small and deeply personal service. And yet everything felt unreal, almost as though I were watching a scene that did not truly belong to my life, as though I were present inside some unbearable film and at the same time unable to feel fully inside my own body.

When we left the chapel, the song "Knockin' on Heaven's Door" began to play. The first notes sounded as we slowly began moving toward the grave. Ahead of me walked the funeral director. Beside him was the man carrying the urn, and directly behind them I followed.

My father-in-law was beside me, and the rest of the family came behind us. The walk through the cemetery felt far longer than it could really have been. There was the soft crunch of our steps beneath us, and although we were all walking together, I felt as though I were making that walk alone, because in that moment my thoughts and feelings had withdrawn so far inward that almost nothing around me seemed fully reachable.

Step by step, we moved forward while sunlight fell through the trees onto the ground. And when we finally arrived, the open grave lay before us, and the sight of it was almost impossible for me to comprehend. That place, that opening in the earth, was now to become the place where his remains would be laid to rest.

At that moment, his favorite song, "Bohemian Rhapsody," filled the air.

As the first notes rose around us, the funeral director slowly began lowering the urn. I was wearing sunglasses because the sun stood high and its brightness fell directly into my face, but behind the dark lenses tears were already running down my cheeks while I tried, with no real success, to understand the reality of what I was seeing. One by one, each of us stepped forward to place a flower into the grave. It was such a simple gesture, almost ritual-like in its simplicity, and yet it carried enormous weight, because every flower felt like one final greeting, a quiet attempt to say what could not really be spoken.

While the music continued in the background, each person remained there for a brief moment before stepping back again, as though that short pause had to hold everything that remained unspoken between love, grief, and farewell.

When the music finally faded, a deep silence spread across the cemetery. It was the kind of silence that feels almost tangible because it leaves no room to avoid the finality of what has just happened. We stood there at the grave within the closest family circle. Some placed another flower there. Others simply remained still, their thoughts with him, their grief too deep or too private for words.

Eventually, the funeral director stepped toward us once more, quietly offered his condolences, and then withdrew, leaving us there so that each of us could say goodbye in our own way. One by one, some family members slowly turned away and began making their way back toward the chapel, because each person had to find their own way of carrying a moment like that. I myself stayed there a while longer, looking at the grave while the realization slowly spread through me that this place was now where his remains had come to rest. That truth did not enter me all at once. It moved more slowly than that, almost unwillingly, and perhaps that was the only reason I could bear it at all.

At some point, that small group too began to disperse. We had planned to sit together for a little while afterward, not to celebrate anything and not to discuss anything, but simply so that no one would have to leave a day like that and go straight home alone. In moments like those, the nearness of the people carrying the same pain becomes important, not because it takes the pain away, but because it offers a kind of quiet support when words no longer have enough strength to do the work on their own.

Chapter 7 – The Puzzle Left Behind

In the weeks after his death, my mind began moving through memories in a way I had never experienced before. It felt less like ordinary remembering and more like some inner process that had begun without my permission, as though a drawer long closed had suddenly been pulled open and all the small, scattered pieces inside it had started shifting at once.

Situations, conversations, expressions, and fragments of ordinary days, things that had once seemed entirely unremarkable and that I had barely thought about at the time because they had simply belonged to our shared life, began returning to me with a force I could not control.

What made it so unsettling was not only that these memories came back, but the way they came back. They did not rise in any clear order, nor did they wait for a suitable moment. Some surfaced without warning and without any obvious trigger at all.

They came while I was sitting in the car, driving roads I knew by heart. They came while I was standing in the kitchen, putting dishes away, my hands occupied with some small ordinary task. They came at night, when I lay awake in bed and should have been sleeping. And it was often in precisely those quiet moments, when everything around me had finally gone still, that my mind seemed to grow louder.

It was as though something inside me was trying desperately to create order in what could no longer be made orderly. I would lie awake for long stretches of time, going back over conversations, sometimes word for word, sometimes glance by glance, sometimes with an almost unbearable concentration on details that had once passed unnoticed.

Over time, one impulse kept rising in me with particular force: the hope that somewhere among those memories there might still be something I had missed, something that, if I could only see it clearly enough now, would finally explain what had happened.

Often it was not the large or obviously dramatic moments that returned, but the smallest things. A sentence spoken in passing. A look that had seemed only briefly unusual at the time. A certain tone in his voice that I may barely have registered then. In hindsight, my mind began examining all of these details differently, almost as though it were holding them up to a new light and asking whether they had meant more than I had understood.

The same question kept returning: had these been signs I simply had not recognized back then?

Some memories changed entirely when viewed from the perspective of loss.

Situations that had once seemed perfectly normal now appeared altered, as though grief itself had shifted the angle from which I looked at them. There had been moments, even then, when I had sensed that something was wrong without being able to name it. It had not been knowledge, not anything firm or provable, but rather a quiet inner unease, a kind of wordless discomfort that settled somewhere beneath the surface and would not fully go away.

At times, I had the impression that he was carrying something within him that I could not quite reach. In those moments, I tried to speak with him. I asked questions. I tried to understand what was going on inside him, and I told him that if something was weighing on him, he could talk to me about it. But so much of it was pushed aside on his end. Some things were simply never spoken about at all, and at times I had the feeling that I had to pull words out of him. Even then, whatever surfaced often remained incomplete, as though certain thoughts would rise only briefly before slipping away again.

Today, I sometimes wonder whether those were the small signs I could not fully make sense of then, signs that only acquired a different weight afterward.

One memory in particular returns with unusual persistence. It is one of those scenes that presses itself deeply into the mind, even though at the time it seemed so ordinary that there was no reason to imagine it would one day matter so much.

It was early in our relationship. We were sitting together at the table, drinking coffee. The day was quiet, one of those simple, unremarkable moments in which two people sit together and talk without anything special needing to happen at all. I still remember the atmosphere of that moment with surprising clarity: the light coming in through the window, the smell of coffee in the air, the ease of the conversation as we spoke about ordinary things, plans, small details from everyday life, thoughts that pass naturally between two people when they are simply spending time together. It was a relaxed, almost gentle moment.

Then he looked at me.

It was not a long look, nor one that seemed especially dramatic at the time. It was only a brief moment in which his attention settled fully on me. His expression was calm, perhaps even a little thoughtful. And then, with a faint smile, he said something that has remained with me ever since:

"You're my final boss."

I still remember the exact way I looked at him when he said it. At first, the sentence sounded almost playful, like something drawn from a video game, and that was precisely why I laughed. In that moment, it did not sound heavy or profound. It sounded more like a teasing remark, something half-serious and half-joking. I asked him what he meant by it, but he only gave a small shrug. I never really received an explanation. The words simply remained there between us, suspended in the space of that conversation, unexplained then and, in truth, unexplained ever since.

At the time, I did not truly understand them, and even later I never found a clear answer. Over the years, I returned to that sentence many times, wondering what he might have meant, trying to place it somewhere in a pattern that would make sense. But that answer never came. Instead, the sentence became one of those puzzle pieces that returns in hindsight and refuses to settle into a fixed meaning.

It may have been more than an offhand remark. It may have been a glimpse of struggles I could not yet see, or a moment in which he tried, in his own way, to put something into words that even he could not fully explain. But it may also have been none of those things. It may simply have been one of those strange, half-playful, half-serious sentences people say without knowing how heavily they might one day be remembered. What makes it so difficult is that hindsight gives even the smallest moments a new gravity, and once loss enters the picture, it becomes almost impossible to look at old memories without asking more of them than they were ever meant to reveal.

And that, maybe, is one of the hardest parts. After such a loss, memory no longer remains neutral. It does not simply preserve what was. It begins to examine, to compare, to search for connections, to look for hidden meanings in moments that once seemed too small to matter. A sentence is no longer just a sentence. A look is no longer just a look. A silence is no longer just a silence. Everything begins to shift under the pressure of what happened afterward.

Sometimes I think about the fact that, from the outside, he seemed to have so many of the things he had wanted in life: a family, a home, people beside him. Someone looking in from the outside might easily have said that his life looked stable. And yet, for all of that, there were evidently thoughts and forces within him that were stronger than what could be seen from the outside. That realization is one of the hardest to carry, because it confronts you with the painful truth that what is visible is not always what is decisive.

There is something deeply unsettling in that.

You begin to understand that love, presence, and shared life do not automatically mean full access to another person's inner world. You can sit beside someone, laugh with them, make plans, build a life together, and still not fully know what battles are taking place inside them. That is not because you did not care enough, or because you did not look closely enough, but because some struggles happen in places no one else can easily enter.

When I think back now to that moment at the table, I can still see him clearly. I can see his face, the faint smile, and hear those words exactly as he said them:

"You're my final boss."

And even now, I cannot say with certainty what they meant. Perhaps he spoke them lightly and without deeper intention. Perhaps they came from some place in him that even he did not fully understand. Perhaps they were simply one of those unusual sentences that would have faded away under other circumstances, had life continued differently. But life did not continue differently, and so the sentence remained. It stayed where so many other small fragments stayed, lodged in memory, refusing to disappear.

I have tried many times to place that memory into the larger picture that began forming after his death. But the more one tries to complete such a puzzle, the clearer it becomes that some pieces are missing. You remember conversations, gestures, and situations that once seemed insignificant, and afterward you begin assigning them greater meaning, as though somewhere among them the answer must still be hiding. The question that follows is always close behind: was there a moment when I could have intervened, said something different, understood more, changed the course of what was to come?

That question can become its own kind of torment. It circles back again and again, taking different shapes but always carrying the same impossible longing. If only I had recognized more. If only I had understood sooner. If only I had known what I know now.

But that way of thinking creates an illusion that the past can still be entered and corrected, as though memory were not only a place of remembering but also a place of repair. Yet it is not. No matter how often you return to the same scenes, they do not open differently. They do not offer new endings. They remain what they were, and you remain the person who moved through them without the knowledge that came only later.

And yet the longing to understand does not simply disappear. It remains because love remains. The need to make sense of what happened is not only a need for explanation. It is also an expression of the bond itself. You search because the person mattered.

You return to those moments because they belonged to a shared life. You turn them over again and again because some part of you still hopes that understanding might lessen the weight of what cannot be changed.

But the longer one follows that path, the clearer it becomes that the puzzle remains incomplete.

Some pieces are missing, and some may remain missing forever. Little by little, you begin to understand that there are questions for which no clear answers will ever come.

Not every situation can be explained afterward, and not every decision can ever be fully understood. Some things remain open, unresolved, beyond interpretation.

There is a particular pain in that kind of incompleteness. Human beings long for coherence. We want causes, reasons, lines that connect one moment to the next in a way that allows us to say, This is how it happened. This is why. This is where everything began to change. But some losses resist that kind of order. They leave behind fragments rather than a full picture, impressions rather than certainty, and memories that illuminate only parts of what was lived.

Maybe that, too, belongs to this kind of loss: that one must learn to live with a puzzle that will never be complete, with memories that remain, with questions that remain, and with a life that, despite everything, goes on. Not because everything has been understood, and not because peace has fully arrived, but because time continues even where understanding does not.

And maybe this is one of the quietest and hardest truths of all: that sometimes you are left not with an answer, but with the task of carrying what will never be fully answered. You carry the memories.

You carry the words that were spoken and the ones that were never spoken. You carry the moments that now seem charged with meaning, and the uncertainty of never knowing exactly how much meaning they truly held.

And somehow, over time, you learn not to solve that puzzle, but to live beside it.

Chapter 8 – The Question Of Guilt

After a suicide, one question almost inevitably rises to the surface, and once it has entered the mind of those left behind, it rarely disappears again in any simple or lasting way.

It returns repeatedly, sometimes quietly, sometimes with overwhelming force, and over time it carves itself so deeply into thought that it begins to feel less like a single question and more like a constant inner presence. It is the question of guilt.

At first, that question appears with a force that is almost impossible to control. It presses its way into your thoughts without being invited, returning at the most different moments of the day, often without warning and often without mercy. Sometimes it arises in the middle of a conversation, while you are trying to focus on something else. Sometimes it intrudes while you are occupied with small ordinary tasks.

And perhaps most often of all, it returns in those quiet moments when everything around you has gone still and your mind begins, once again, to move back through memory. In those moments, an inner dialogue begins that circles endlessly around the same point. It is a question that cannot be answered easily, because it is not really searching for facts so much as possibilities. It asks not only what happened, but what might have happened differently. Could I have prevented it?

That thought almost automatically sends the mind backward. Memories rise again. Conversations return before the inner eye. Situations that once seemed entirely ordinary are suddenly revisited from a completely different angle. What had once simply belonged to the flow of everyday life now begins to look altered in hindsight.

You remember things that were said in passing, things you may not have fully understood at the time. You think back to looks that now seem heavier than they did in the moment they occurred. You begin revisiting small situations, as though trying to discover in them a meaning that escaped you then. The mind begins examining memory almost like an investigator, trying to gather scattered details and fit them into a coherent picture. Conversations are replayed.

Words are weighed again. Silences, gestures, and tones of voice begin to seem charged with new significance.

And with all of this comes the recurring impression that maybe, back then, there was something you should have seen, something you should have understood, something that should somehow have alerted you to the danger that was already unfolding beneath the surface.

It is a process that is almost impossible to control, precisely because it is driven by the longing to find a point in the past at which everything might still have been able to change. You begin imagining how certain situations might have unfolded if you had reacted differently. Maybe there had been a moment that called for a different conversation, closer attention, or an earlier recognition that something had changed.

And the longer you follow those thoughts, the more possibilities appear, possibilities that seem persuasive only because they are being viewed from the knowledge you now carry. And that is exactly where the difficulty lies.

All of these reflections arise from the perspective of what is known now. But back then, that knowledge did not exist.

Back then, so much of what now seems charged with meaning was still woven into the fabric of ordinary life, where not every remark sounds like a warning and not every silence can be recognized for what it may conceal. Hindsight creates patterns that were not visible in the moment, and because of that, it can make the past feel more readable than it really was.

Over time, one begins to recognize that people rarely show everything that is happening inside them. Many thoughts remain unspoken. Many fears and doubts are never fully shared. Many struggles unfold in silence, without the people closest to them ever truly seeing the full extent of what is taking place. Especially those who are battling something deep within themselves often carry those thoughts alone for a very long time.

They try to make sense of their feelings. They search for solutions. They hope, maybe, that something within them will shift or ease. And not everything they carry can be put into language, even if someone beside them is willing to listen. Not everything is spoken aloud. Not everything is explained. And even between people who love one another deeply, there are inner realities that remain partly hidden.

This realization begins, slowly and often painfully, to change the way one looks at the question of guilt. But that change does not happen all at once. In the beginning, it can feel almost impossible to accept that love alone is not always enough to end another person's inner struggle. One wants to believe that closeness, understanding, conversation, and care possess a power great enough to lead someone back out of darkness. One wants to believe that being there, truly being there, ought to make the decisive difference.

And yet reality often proves more complex than that hope allows. You can listen. You can stay. You can ask questions, offer help, try to open a door. But help can only reach as far as another person is willing, or able, to let it reach. If someone cannot share what is happening inside them, or does not know how to name it, then part of that reality remains invisible to everyone else, no matter how much they care.

This understanding does not arrive as a single clear moment of truth. It develops slowly, over weeks and months, and sometimes over far longer than that. Because the question of guilt has a particular power: it keeps drawing you back into the past. It sends you back to moments you study once more, as though somewhere among those memories there must still be an answer waiting to be found.

You analyze conversations, revisit situations, and try to read between the lines. You ask yourself whether there might have been a different word, a different conversation, a different response, or a different decision that could have changed the course of what happened.

But the longer one follows that path, the clearer it often becomes that a human life is never made up of isolated moments that can simply be rearranged from the outside.

A life is the result of countless experiences, inner processes, thoughts, wounds, and histories, most of which are known only in fragments by the people standing nearby.

Over time, I began to understand that not every decision another person makes lies in the hands of those around them. As much as one might wish otherwise, there are limits to what one person can do for another. Maybe more time could have been gained, a moment delayed, or something, in some small way, could have unfolded differently.

And yet, over time, the belief that everything could have been prevented begins to lose some of its certainty. That realization does not erase the questions. It does not make them disappear entirely. Even later, there are still moments when the question of guilt returns, whether through memories, through particular conversations, or through meeting other people who have lived through something similar. But the way one looks at that question does begin to change.

Slowly, one begins to understand that responsibility has many forms. We carry responsibility for our words, for our decisions, and for the ways we move through relationships. But we do not carry responsibility for every decision another person makes.

That realization does not remove the pain, nor does it dissolve grief. But it can help, little by little, to loosen the grip of guilt and allow the gaze to turn, however hesitantly, toward what still lies ahead.

Chapter 9 – Silence

After the funeral, a kind of silence settled over everything, one unlike anything I had ever known before. In the days leading up to it, there had still been movement all around me. People had come and gone, conversations had continued, decisions had needed to be made, and there had been a constant stream of practical matters that demanded attention.

The phone rang more often than usual, messages kept coming in, and again and again people reached out to ask how we were doing. Friends, family members, and acquaintances wanted to know how I was coping, how the children were doing, and whether there was anything we needed in order to get through everyday life. Much of this concern was sincere, and in those first days it mattered to feel that we had not been forgotten, that people were thinking of us and trying, in whatever way they could, to come close to something for which there were really no adequate words.

I could sense how carefully many people were searching for what to say, even though situations like this make it painfully clear that the "right" words do not truly exist. Sometimes it was only a brief phone call, sometimes a message, and sometimes nothing more than a single sentence - "I'm thinking of you" - and yet even that could feel, at least for a moment, like a small form of steadiness. In that early phase, it almost seemed as though the world around us had slowed down a little. People moved with more caution. Conversations were gentler. Many tried, in their own way, to express sympathy, closeness, or care.

For a short time, there was the feeling that the loss had not only shattered us, but had also caused something in the people around us to pause.

And yet, little by little, that began to change. The messages became fewer. The calls came less often. The first weeks passed, and one by one, people returned to their own routines, to their work, to their families, and to all the small obligations and familiar structures from which ordinary life is made. And of course that was understandable.

The world cannot remain suspended forever. Other people's lives continue, as they must.

Days keep moving forward, responsibilities do not disappear, and the rhythm of normal life slowly reasserts itself. Still, even though I understood this with my mind, it often felt as though my own world had stopped exactly where it had been broken.

While a sense of normality gradually returned everywhere around me, something inside me remained fixed in place. What was left there was not simply sadness, but a wide inner emptiness and a silence so deep that it is difficult to describe without diminishing it.

Outwardly, life began, in some ways, to resemble itself again. I got up in the mornings, took care of the children, did the things that had to be done, and tried somehow to give each day a shape that was manageable. From the outside, it may well have looked as though things were slowly finding their way back into some recognizable order.

But inwardly, nothing had returned to what it had been. So much of what I did felt less like living and more like functioning. I moved through the day because I had to. I carried out the tasks in front of me because there was no alternative.

But everything inside me felt quieter, heavier, and more distant than before, as though an invisible dividing line had been drawn through my life, separating everything irrevocably into a before and an after. Everywhere I looked, the world continued in ways that seemed almost impossible to reconcile with what had happened. I saw people in the street, heard fragments of conversation in stores, watched families out together, and noticed how naturally life continued to unfold for everyone else. People laughed, made plans, bought groceries, met friends, and went about their days as if the structure of the world had remained intact.

And I stood in the middle of that same world, often feeling as though some part of me was still standing at the exact point where everything had changed. It was as if time had resumed for everyone else, while within me a part of it had remained trapped in that moment of rupture. Even within the family, there came a time when we spoke less openly about what had happened. Not because it had become less important, and not because the loss itself had receded, but perhaps because each of us was trying, in a deeply personal way, to survive it.

Everyone carried their own thoughts, memories, and emotions inwardly, and perhaps that is one of the strangest things about grief: several people can lose the same person, and yet no two people will move through that loss in the same way. We were connected by the same absence, and yet each of us had to find a separate path through it. That was not a sign of distance or lack of love. It was simply the nature of grief itself, which rarely takes the same shape in two people at once.

Over time, I also began to sense a growing uncertainty in the people around me. Some no longer knew whether they should bring the subject up again. Others may have feared reopening wounds or saying the wrong thing. And so, gradually, it became quieter. The questions came less often. Conversations grew more careful, and at times I even had the impression that some people no longer quite knew how to be with me. Maybe it was uncertainty, fear, or simply helplessness in the face of something for which there are no instructions.

But even as the outer conversations became fewer, my inner life did not grow quieter in the same way.

My thoughts remained, and my memories returned again and again, often without warning.

Sometimes they appeared in the middle of an ordinary task, sometimes in moments of stillness, and sometimes exactly when I least expected them. A song on the radio could be enough. So could a place we had once been together, or a sentence overheard somewhere that suddenly opened a door inside me.

In those moments, I began to understand that grief does not disappear in the way people sometimes imagine. It does not simply fade and leave nothing behind. What it does, perhaps, is change form. It moves. It shifts. It returns differently. But it remains.

And within that silence, something else also began to emerge. It was not peace, at least not yet, and it was not acceptance in any simple sense. It felt more like the beginning of a new phase, one shaped less by the noise of the first days and more by the quiet persistence of inner reality. The time of constant calls, immediate reactions, and outward movement was slowly receding, and in its place came a stretch of life in which I had to begin understanding, in a deeper and less avoidable way, that life would continue - but that it would never again be exactly what it had once been.

That realization did not come all at once. It unfolded slowly, almost imperceptibly, as so many things in grief do. It was part of a larger process, one of understanding and, in some fragile way, of continuing to live. Because at some point I began to see that this silence was not only a sign of what had been lost. It was also the space in which I would have to learn how to live with what had happened.

It was the place in which memory, pain, absence, and the first hesitant movements of life beginning again had to exist side by side.

Part III: The Road Ahead

Chapter 10 – What Remains

Over time, I came to understand something about grief that no book, no well-meaning guide, and no outside observer could ever have taught me in quite this way. I did not learn it from theory, and I did not find it in the comforting words of people who tried to ease my pain.

I learned it in my own life, in my own body, in the structure of my own days and nights. I learned it through an experience I never would have chosen for myself and that nevertheless became part of my story, whether I wanted it to or not.

Before this loss, I had already known what it meant to lose people. There had been deaths in my family, farewells in my wider circle, and like anyone else, I already knew on some level that loss belongs to life, even if most of us prefer to keep that knowledge at a distance for as long as we can. Some people had died after illness. Others had died through accidents. Others simply because life eventually reaches the point at which it ends.

Each of those losses had left traces. Each had hurt, and none of them had been easy. And yet none of them had felt like this.

Maybe the difference lies in the fact that suicide does not only take a person away. It also shakes the inner structure of the life left behind. It is not only the pain of someone no longer being there. It is also the shock of the manner in which they left, the force of a reality that is difficult to grasp not only emotionally, but mentally as well. Suddenly, it is not only a person who is missing. Something else is lost too: the quiet, unspoken assumption that life will continue in a certain recognizable form.

There was a time when I believed grief became smaller with time, shrinking little by little until it remained only as a faded memory at the edge of life. I imagined it as a wound that was first open, then slowly healed, and finally became nothing more than a scar, something you might touch from time to time, but that no longer shaped the whole of your days. I thought grief was a condition one eventually left behind, like a very difficult period that, years later, one could look back on and say had been survived.

Today, I know that grief does not work that way.

It does not disappear simply because time passes. It does not submit to the ideas other people sometimes have about it, and it does not follow any clean emotional schedule at the end of which a person arrives at closure. It changes, yes. With time, it may take on a different shape, appear in different ways, and occupy a different place in life, but it does not simply leave. In the beginning, it stands at the center of everything and takes the air from the room. Later, it may no longer sit in every corner of daily life in quite the same way, but it remains there nonetheless, sometimes quiet, sometimes almost invisible, and sometimes suddenly so close again that it feels as though no time has passed at all.

When I think back now to the time immediately after his death, I do not remember only the shock, only the emptiness, or only the many practical matters that seemed to come crashing down on me all at once. More than anything, I remember the questions that lodged themselves in my mind and returned again and again, no matter how much I longed for peace. They were not questions that stayed politely in the background. They followed me through the day and into the night, surfacing whenever there was enough silence for them to make themselves heard.

One of those nights remains especially clear in my memory. The house had long since grown quiet. The children were asleep, and outside there was only that deep nighttime stillness that houses sometimes seem to hold when everything has finally come to rest. I was sitting alone in the kitchen. The light above the table was still on, and in front of me sat a cup of tea that had gone cold without my even noticing. In moments like that, there was nothing left to distract me. No conversations. No tasks. No sounds from the day. There were only my thoughts.

And then they began again.

Why did this happen? Should I have noticed something? Could I have done something differently? Was there a moment when something might still have been possible?

Those questions did not come once. They returned over and over again. They came in the night when I could not sleep. They came in the car when I was alone. They came while I was doing completely ordinary things, shopping, folding laundry, wiping down the kitchen, moving through the practical motions of life while something else inside me continued asking for answers. Again and again, they slipped themselves between the thoughts of the day.

For a long time, I believed I would have to answer those questions in order to find any peace at all. But the more I looked back, the more difficult it became to separate memory from interpretation. The more I turned things over in my mind, the less certain I became about where recollection ended and hindsight began.

With time, I also came to understand that what remains after a suicide is not only a set of questions, but often a collection of images. What remains is not only the fact that someone has died, but also what one has seen, read, heard, and lived through around that death.

Certain impressions settle so deeply into memory that they seem to remain in the body as much as in the mind, and they are not impressions one chooses. They return when they want to return, sometimes without warning and sometimes with such force that, for a moment, the present seems to give way beneath them.

I remember, for example, a moment in the car several months after his death. The radio was playing quietly in the background when suddenly a song came on that we had once listened to often. In that instant, it felt as though a door had opened somewhere inside me. For a brief moment, I was no longer only in the present. I was also inside a memory, and both realities seemed to exist at once.

That, too, is something I now know: grief does not follow a fixed plan. It does not move neatly, logically, or fairly. A person does not simply pass from one phase into the next as though checking off emotional steps in the correct order. Grief moves more like something living. It changes, retreats, returns, grows quieter, and then, without warning, becomes loud again.

There are days when life feels lighter, when the weight is not gone but less immediate, less sharp. And then there are other days when something very small is enough to bring you inwardly back to a place you believed you had already moved beyond. I no longer think of that as falling backward. I think it is simply part of grief itself.

Another thing I gradually came to understand is that grief is not made only of pain. At some point, something else begins to mingle with it: memory, and with memory, an ongoing relationship to someone who is no longer physically here. Maybe that is one reason grief is so full of contradiction. It hurts because something is missing, and at the same time it holds on because the bond does not simply end.

Over time, I have learned that continuing to live does not mean leaving the loss behind. It means learning to live with it, without allowing it to dominate every single moment of existence. That does not happen all at once, nor does it happen in a straight line. It happens slowly, unevenly, and often without one noticing it at first.

For me now, grief no longer means only loss. It also means memory, change, connection, and the difficult art of living with something I never wanted. It means understanding that pain and life can exist at the same time. It means allowing laughter to return without believing that love has been diminished. And it means knowing that a person can be absent and yet still remain, in a quiet and inward way, present within you.

None of this takes away the weight of the loss. It does not make the reality gentler, and it does not undo what was shattered. But maybe it does make one thing possible: that at some point, you no longer look only at what has been broken, but also at what, despite everything, can still be carried forward.

And maybe that is my most honest answer now to the question of what grief means to me.

It has not disappeared.

But it has changed.

Chapter 11 – Going On

There was a moment, several months after his death, that was marked by nothing extraordinary on the surface. It was not a date that burned itself into memory, nor an event one could later point to and call a turning point. It was, rather, one of those days that appear entirely unremarkable from the outside and are therefore easily overlooked, even though inwardly they set something in motion that is only fully understood much later.

I was at a playground with my children. They were running, laughing, moving through their own small world with that natural certainty children have, a world in which the past and the future carry little weight and in which only the present moment exists in its fullness. I was sitting on a bench a little off to the side, not truly separate, but not entirely in the middle of things either, and for a while I simply watched them. I did not say anything. I did not intervene. I was not even consciously trying to understand what I was witnessing. I was simply there.

And as I sat there, something began to register in me, though it did not arrive as a sharp realization.

It felt more like the quiet noticing of something that had already been there for some time, something I had not yet truly allowed myself to see.

Life was continuing.

Not with a dramatic shift, not with the clear feeling of a new beginning, and not with any kind of soothing clarity. It was continuing in a way that felt almost indifferent, as though it had nothing to do with me at all. It did not pause. It did not ask whether I was ready. It did not wait for permission. It simply kept moving, the way life always does, regardless of what a single person has lived through.

People passed by me, talking to one another. Children played. Someone laughed loudly. Something fell to the ground somewhere nearby. A bicycle rolled past. Conversations began and ended. And all of this happened without the world appearing to change in any noticeable way, even as I felt with complete certainty that something inside me had shifted so fundamentally that it could no longer be named in simple terms.

And in that moment, a question appeared.

It did not arrive loudly or urgently. It came more carefully than that, almost as though it were hesitant itself, as though it first needed to find its place before daring to be fully spoken:

What happens now? How does life go on from here?

It was not a new question. It had been with me before. But for a long time it had been covered over by everything that comes immediately after loss, by that strange state in which one functions without really understanding how it is possible to survive another day, and in which one clings to routines because everything else feels like too much.

But that afternoon, sitting on that bench while my children played and life continued around me, I understood something different about that question. I understood that it was not going to disappear. It was not a question that would one day simply be answered and then laid to rest. It would remain. It would change. It would return in different moments and in different forms, sometimes quietly in the background, sometimes all at once, startlingly present.

I am a mother.

That had never been merely a description of my role. It had always also meant responsibility. But during that time, the meaning of that responsibility deepened, because it no longer meant only being there for my children in the ordinary sense. It meant giving them steadiness inside a reality that for a long time I myself could barely grasp. Something fundamental was missing, something that could not be replaced and yet continued to resonate in every moment.

I watched their lives continue. I watched them laugh, play, ask questions, grow, and move forward in the natural rhythm of childhood, untouched by many of the inner fractures that defined my own experience. They were developing in their own time, in their own way, regardless of what had happened. And there was something about that that felt both comforting and almost unbearable, because it revealed with painful clarity that life does not stop, not even when part of you feels as though everything inside has gone still.

And it was at exactly that point that an inner conflict began to form, though I did not immediately recognize it as such. It developed slowly, almost imperceptibly, through thoughts that came and went, feelings I could not immediately name, and moments in which something felt off without my being able to explain why.

One part of me knew that life goes on, that there is in fact no alternative, because time does not stop and because everything around us continues to move whether we are ready for it or not.

But another part of me wondered whether it was even allowed.

Was it right to laugh again? Was it right to look forward to something? To make plans beyond the next day? To begin, inwardly, to move in the direction of a future, when something so final had happened?

These questions did not come in the form of fixed convictions. They felt more like a quiet hesitation, a kind of inward holding back that did not feel consciously chosen so much as simply present, as though something inside me were saying that moving forward was not self-evident, but something that first had to be permitted.

It took me some time to understand what lay beneath that feeling, because it does not show itself directly and there are no ready-made words for it. It is more like a silent form of loyalty, one that is never spoken aloud, one that sets down no rules and yet can be incredibly powerful, because it influences the shape of one's life without being immediately recognized. It alters decisions. It dulls certain emotions. It quietly narrows what feels possible, not because one consciously declares that to be the case, but because something inside has linked moving forward with leaving behind.

It is the feeling that movement itself is a kind of loss. That taking a step forward is, at the same time, taking a step away. That thought alone can be enough to keep a person standing still, not because they have clearly decided to do so, but because everything else feels wrong.

There were many moments in which I caught myself holding back, not fully allowing certain things in, not fully stepping toward possibilities that were there. And it was not exactly fear of what might come next. It was something quieter and harder to grasp than fear, something that worked steadily in the background and made life smaller, more careful, more muted, not because it had to be that way, but because I was shaping it that way without fully realizing I was doing it.

And that is where a danger lies, one that often becomes visible only when you step back far enough to observe yourself honestly. Because you begin to notice that your life is growing quieter, narrower, more cautious, not out of necessity, but because you are unconsciously arranging it that way.

The longer I sat with this, the clearer it became to me that this could not be the right way forward. Not for me, and not for my children. Life does not wait for readiness. Time does not stand still. Growth does not pause. My children are growing every day, sometimes in ways so small they are easy to miss, and sometimes in ways that are unmistakable. And in that growth there is something unstoppable, something that keeps moving regardless of what has happened. I am part of that movement, whether I feel ready for it or not.

I cannot change the past. I cannot undo what has happened. I cannot force answers into existence, and I cannot fully understand everything. But there is still something left that I can influence: the way I go on living with what has happened.

And that is not a decision made once and for all. It is a decision that has to be made again and again, in small moments, in ordinary situations, in thoughts that come and go, in feelings that shift, and in the quiet ways one begins to give oneself room again, even when doing so feels strange at first, or even wrong.

Moving forward does not mean forgetting. It does not mean that something has been resolved, or that loss eventually becomes light or easy to carry. It means learning to bear something that will never fully dissolve, because it has become part of your history. It does not disappear. It changes. It becomes quieter. It shifts. And still, it remains.

It means that pain does not simply leave; it changes its place. It no longer determines every single moment, and yet it does not vanish. Instead, it begins to exist alongside what is still growing, what is still unfolding, what still continues, despite all the times one believed development itself was no longer possible.

And that is one of the hardest truths to put into words, because it is not a clear either-or. It is not over, and it is not new. It is a coexistence in which something is missing and something else continues living, in which memory remains and life still moves, and in which both of these truths exist at once without canceling each other out.

I came to understand that the task is not to resolve this state or make it fit into a form that can be explained neatly. The task is to accept it, not in the sense of approving of it, but in the sense of recognizing it as reality, because there is nothing powerful enough to undo it completely. And it is there, in that difficult recognition, that something begins. Not a dramatic step. Not a declared new beginning. More like a quiet continuation, a movement that is not fully planned and not always consciously chosen, but that happens because life itself keeps moving, because time passes, and because things continue to emerge even after long stretches in which one believed nothing new could ever arise again.

Moving forward, then, does not mean leaving someone behind. It does not mean detaching or erasing or abandoning what was. It means carrying that person differently, not visibly, not tangibly, but still in a way that is deeply felt, in thoughts, in memories, and in moments that arrive without warning and disappear again before they can be held onto.

And maybe that is the deepest truth of it: that there is no clear ending, no simple point at which one chapter closes and another begins. There is only this ongoing in-between, this continuous movement through a life that has been changed and cannot be changed back. Sometimes that movement is conscious. Sometimes it happens only because there is no alternative. And maybe that is exactly why moving forward is not betrayal, abandonment, or a failure of love.

It is life itself.

A life that does not ask whether you are ready, but continues all the same, and in which, step by step, you begin to find your place again, not the place you once had, but the one that is possible now.

Chapter 12 – What Stays

For a long time, I believed there had to be a point at which everything would somehow fall into place. I imagined there must one day come a moment when my thoughts would stop circling, when what had happened could be brought into a form that would at least feel somewhat coherent, not in the sense of being fully understood, but in the sense that inwardly I might finally stop searching, stop questioning, stop taking everything apart.

That idea stayed with me for a long time. Sometimes it was conscious; at other times it remained quieter, more like an unspoken expectation somewhere in the background of my mind. It was the hope that there must be something like an ending to all of this, some state in which what had happened would still remain part of my story, but would no longer keep reaching so insistently into the present, no longer echo through every moment, and no longer make itself known in so many invisible ways. I thought there might come a time when it would settle, become quieter, and eventually even make room for something that felt like peace.

But over time, that idea changed.

It did not change suddenly, and it was not undone by one clear realization. It shifted more slowly than that, through many small moments in which it became clear to me that there are some experiences that cannot be resolved, no matter how deeply one longs for them to be, no matter how often one tries to give them shape, a beginning, an explanation, an end.

At some point, I began to understand that this story was not something I would one day leave behind. The task was not to get past it. The task was to live with it. And that difference is larger than it first sounds, because it means there is no clean break, no point at which one thing ends and something entirely new begins. What it means instead is that what was does not disappear, but gradually becomes woven into what is.

That understanding did not come all at once. It developed slowly, almost unnoticed, in the middle of days filled with responsibility, decisions, and the attempt to bring structure back into a life that for a long time had felt inwardly unsettled, even while something remained inside it that could not be put in order.

It was often in the quietest moments that this became most visible to me. Not in the dramatic or obviously difficult situations, but in those seemingly ordinary moments that had changed only because I had changed, because something in me was no longer what it had once been.

I remember one evening in particular that, seen from the outside, would have looked entirely unremarkable. It was nothing more than a moment on the couch. There was no deep conversation, no heavy subject, no visible crisis. It was simply that quiet kind of closeness that exists when two people know one another well, when they feel safe in each other's presence, and when words are not always necessary for closeness to be felt.

He was sitting beside me, leaning slightly forward, his hands clasped together, and for a brief moment I had the feeling that something was moving inside him, something I could not reach, could not name, something that did not reveal itself and yet was undeniably there, almost like a shadow that only becomes visible if you look very closely, and even then cannot really be grasped.

I remember looking at him and sensing that there was more in him than he was saying, more than he wanted to show, and yet I did not ask anything in that moment. It was not because I did not care. It was because it did not feel right to force open a space he himself had not opened.

Today, I often think back to moments like that, not as clear memories with fixed meaning, but as fragments that feel different in retrospect because I now know there were things I saw without being able to understand them.

There are things I know that hardly anyone else knew, not because they emerged through many conversations, and not because I was gradually given a complete picture, but because there was one night that has remained unlike all the others in my memory. It was one of those nights when sleep does not come, when conversations go deeper than they usually do, perhaps because darkness creates room for what daylight cannot hold.

That night, he told me something.

Not in detail. Not in a way that explained everything. Not in a form that could be neatly understood. He spoke through tears, in words that did not seem intended to make full sense, but simply to be spoken aloud at all, as though something had risen to the surface for a brief moment that otherwise never found room to exist.

I know what he experienced.

But I do not know everything.

I do not know the full details. I do not know every name, every connection, every thread that might have allowed those fragments to become a complete picture. There is nothing I can hold in my hands and arrange into understanding. Nothing that can be fully ordered in retrospect, because there is a boundary there that he himself never crossed.

And that is one of the hardest things to endure.

Because it means that even in the greatest closeness, not everything is accessible. It means that there are parts of a person's life they carry alone, even when they are deeply loved, and that this incompleteness remains even after the person themselves is gone.

He took that part of his life with him.

And I remain here with what I know.

And with what I will never know.

To live with this story, then, also means learning to live with not knowing. It means living with those open spaces that cannot be closed, with those thoughts that sometimes return and do not lead to answers, but only to a quieter acceptance of what cannot be changed.

At the same time, it is often the ordinary moments that reveal most clearly how much has changed, because life continues, because children laugh, because conversations happen, because decisions have to be made, and because through all of it something remains present that cannot be seen and yet is always there.

It is as though this story sits at the table with me, not loudly, not in a way that overshadows everything, but as something quietly present while I laugh, while I function, while I try to be strong, even when I am not consciously thinking about it.

In the beginning, I resisted that. I wanted it to become less. I wanted it to disappear. I wanted to arrive, at some point, in a place where everything felt lighter again, and I kept wondering when that moment would come, the moment so many people speak of when they say it gets better, time helps, and you will learn how to deal with it.

But what I have experienced is not a simple becoming better.

What I have experienced is a form of change that is much harder to describe, because it does not mean that something disappears. It means that one's relationship to it changes. The force of it softens. Daily life begins to take shape again. And at the same time, something stays that does not dissolve.

You do not learn to leave it behind.

You learn to carry it with you.

And maybe that is the deeper truth of it, that both things can exist at once. That life continues. That there can be moments of lightness. That there can be laughter. That there can still be a future. And that at the very same time, something is missing that will never return.

Not as a contradiction.

But as reality.

And maybe that is the point at which something begins to shift, not because an answer has been found, but because one accepts that there will not be an answer for everything, and that life continues nonetheless. Not because everything has been clarified, but because life moves whether one is ready or not.

To live with this story, then, does not mean overcoming it. It means accepting it as part of one's path, not out of agreement, not because one would ever have chosen it, and not because it defines everything, but because it belongs now to the shape of one's life.

And maybe there is a quiet kind of strength in that, one that has nothing to do with control and everything to do with enduring what cannot be changed, and continuing even while knowing that there are things that will stay forever.

Chapter 13 – If You Are Here

If you are here, then you have already traveled farther than can be measured in pages. The path behind you is not made of chapter breaks or numbers, but of moments that were hard to bear, of thoughts that have circled without rest, and of feelings that refused to settle into anything simple or easy to name.

The fact that you have stayed with this book until here means more than it might seem at first, because this is not the kind of story one simply reads and sets aside unchanged. It is something a person moves through, step by step, sometimes steadily, sometimes haltingly, and sometimes with the need to stop for a while because what is being named feels too close, too familiar, or too honest to take in all at once.

You may have read these pages because you yourself lost someone to suicide. You may have been searching for a way to understand something that does not fully allow itself to be understood.

You may have been looking for language for an experience that so often resists language altogether. And by now, you may already know that many of the things people say in the face of such a loss do not truly reach it, do not hold it, and do not carry the weight of what they are meant to comfort.

Or you may have come to this book for another reason. You may be walking beside someone who is living with this kind of loss, and you wanted to understand what happens inside a person when life changes from one moment to the next without warning, without preparation, and without any clear passage from one reality into another.

Whatever brought you here, and whatever story you brought with you while reading these pages, something has kept you here. Something allowed you to continue, even when continuing was not easy. And maybe that something was this quiet sense, somewhere between the lines, that you are not alone with what you think or feel, even if it has often seemed exactly that way.

You may know those moments in which you try to sort through your thoughts and realize that nothing inside you arranges itself cleanly. There is no neat sequence, no emotional order in which one feeling makes room for the next. Instead, everything seems to exist at once, grief, anger, guilt, longing, exhaustion, disbelief, and those strange stretches of numbness in which you feel both too much and not enough. None of it arrives one after the other. It gathers all at once, and because of that, it can feel impossible to understand yourself clearly even while you are living inside your own experience.

I have known that kind of inner confusion as well.

I have searched, questioned, turned things over in my mind, and tried to fit together pieces that refused to form a complete picture. For a long time, I hoped I might eventually reach a point where everything would at least begin to feel somewhat coherent, because it would have been easier if there had been one clear reason, one explanation that could be named, held, and understood.

But the longer I lived with these questions, the more I came to recognize that some things do not yield to even the most relentless search for meaning. That is not because one has looked too little, overlooked something simple, or failed to love deeply enough. It is because there are realities that remain incomplete no matter how often we return to them, and losses that resist being shaped into a final, satisfying answer.

You may know that place too, the place where you realize you are moving in circles, thinking the same thoughts, asking the same questions, and turning over the same possibilities, only to arrive once again at the same unresolved edge. And then, at some point, there comes a quieter kind of understanding, one that does not feel like resolution at all, but more like the recognition that resolution may never fully come. What remains then is not an answer, but the difficult realization that some things stay open, and that there may never be a single thought strong enough to gather everything together and make it entirely clear.

If you have lost someone to suicide, then you may know how impossible it can feel to sort what remains into separate categories. Grief in this form is never only grief. It is also anger, bewilderment, guilt, longing, and those moments of pure exhaustion in which you are simply tired of carrying something that does not dissolve.

You may also know what it is like when the people around you do not quite know how to meet you there. They grow careful. Hesitant. Quiet. Sometimes they say things that are well meant and still somehow fail to land. Sometimes they say nothing at all, because language fails them and they are afraid of saying the wrong thing. That does not always mean a lack of care. And yet it can still deepen the loneliness.

One of the hardest things about this kind of loss is the way it can leave a person feeling both held and isolated at the same time, surrounded by others, and yet inwardly alone with something that cannot be fully shared. At some point, you may even have begun adapting yourself to that reality. You may have started saying less, holding more back, softening your thoughts before speaking them, because you realized how difficult they are to carry, not only for you, but often for those around you as well. Not everyone can remain in that depth for very long.

And still, even if it sometimes feels as though you must carry all of this entirely on your own, that is not the whole truth. There are others who have walked similar roads, others who have asked questions like yours, others who have also tried to bring their lives, after such a break, into some form that feels at least possible to live in, even if it never again feels the way it once did. No two of those paths are identical. There is no correct version of grief, no timetable that proves you are progressing as you should, and no emotional measure by which your way of carrying this can be judged.

At the same time, there is something that cannot be avoided, however deeply one resists it. Life continues. It does not continue as some grand decision or as a satisfying next step, and it certainly does not arrive like a reward for having suffered in the proper way. It continues more quietly and more relentlessly than that, simply as the fact that time moves, days follow one another, and the world does not wait for us to become ready for the lives we are still inside.

That continuation does not mean everything becomes easier, nor does it mean that answers suddenly appear where none existed before. It means only that time passes, that small things begin to shift, and that movement keeps happening, often so quietly that one notices it only afterward. Sometimes you realize, almost with surprise, that something in you has moved a little. You may already have had a moment in which you allowed a thought that once would have felt impossible. For an instant, your mind may not have looked only backward, but also forward, not because you had planned it and not because you felt ready, but because the thought arose and could no longer be fully pushed away.

This is often how change begins, not with a dramatic turning point, but with a quieter internal shift that no one else may even notice. It is not loud or sudden, but it is real. And maybe what it reveals most clearly is that inner stillness, however absolute it may feel, is not a permanent state.

There comes a point at which the question changes, even if it does not disappear. It is no longer only "Why did this happen?" or "What did I miss?" It also becomes "What now?" and "How does life go on from here?" Those questions are not answered once and for all. They stay. They evolve. They change shape as your life changes shape.

You may also have wondered whether you are even allowed to go on. Whether it is right to laugh again, to look forward to something, to make plans that extend beyond the next day, or to let yourself move inwardly toward a future while something so final has happened.

Those thoughts are often quieter than grief itself, but they can be just as powerful, because they determine how much life you permit yourself to feel, how much room you allow yourself to take up again, and how much movement you can tolerate in yourself without feeling as though you are betraying what has been lost.

But your continuing does not erase what happened, nor does it diminish the love that was there. It does not replace the person you lost, and it does not ask you to loosen your hold on what mattered. It simply means that your life is still unfolding, even now, and that what happened remains part of that life rather than something outside it. In that sense, movement is not betrayal, nor is it disloyalty or forgetting. It is simply the reality of being alive after something has happened that changed everything.

You can resist that movement for a long time by withdrawing, withholding yourself from life, and refusing what still wants to grow. But even then, life continues underneath the resistance. That is not because it is fair, and certainly not because it feels easy. It is because life itself does not remain still. Whether we are ready or not, it keeps moving, and it carries us with it in ways we do not always choose consciously.

What can change is not whether life continues, but how you meet its continuation. You can stand inwardly against every shift in yourself, or you can begin, slowly and often reluctantly, to acknowledge that movement is already happening. And that is where something begins to change. Not all at once, and not through one decisive act of will, but through the quieter process of allowing your life to become visible to you again, not apart from what happened, but alongside it.

So if there is anything left at the end of this book, it is not an easy message, a final answer, or a sentence large enough to gather every pain into meaning. What remains is something quieter than that: the understanding that your life has not stopped, even if a part of you still feels as though it did. It is already moving, whether or not you feel ready to move with it. And that movement is not something that will begin someday in the future. It has already begun. It is already present in every day you have endured, every thought you have survived, and every small inward shift that may hardly be visible and is still part of this process.

The deeper question, then, is not whether you are on this path.

You already are.

The question is whether, at some point, you stop resisting that fact so completely and begin allowing it to belong to your life. Not because any of this is easy, and not because it feels fair, but because life moves in only one direction. And maybe the quiet truth beneath all of this is that continuing is not something you must first begin. It is something you are already doing.

A Note To Readers

This book is rooted in personal experience, reflection, and lived reality. It grew out of one individual path through grief after suicide, and it speaks from within a space that many bereaved people know all too well: a space shaped by shock, uncertainty, emotional intensity, and questions that often remain unanswered far longer than anyone expects.

The loss of a loved one to suicide is one of those experiences that can alter life at its core. For many people, what follows is not grief alone. It may also include confusion, guilt, anger, helplessness, numbness, and a profound sense of speechlessness in the face of what has happened. These responses are not unusual. They belong to a deeply personal inner process, one that can unfold differently for every person living through it.

This book does not attempt to prescribe one universal way through such an experience. There is no single path through grief, no fixed sequence of emotions, and no moment at which certain feelings become "right" or "wrong." What is shared in these pages reflects one personal way of living through such a loss. It may offer recognition, open certain thoughts, or help give language to feelings that can otherwise remain difficult to name. At the same time, it cannot speak equally to every life situation, because every person brings their own history, relationships, and emotional realities into grief.

For that reason, the purpose of this book is not to provide solutions in any final or absolute sense. Its deeper intention is to create understanding. It is meant to make visible that people who go through this kind of loss are not alone with what they think, feel, fear, or carry. Many survivors describe a powerful sense of isolation after suicide loss. In many places, this is still a subject that is rarely spoken about openly. Some people do not know how to respond when they hear of such a loss. Others want to help, but cannot find words that feel adequate. That uncertainty can leave those who are grieving feeling even more alone than they already do.

One of the hopes behind this book is therefore to open space for thoughts and emotions that often remain unspoken. Anger, guilt, helplessness, deep sorrow, inner conflict, and emotional exhaustion can all be part of this path. They are not signs of weakness or failure. They are expressions of an experience that has changed life in a fundamental way.

And maybe my story can make one thing visible as well: however isolating suicide loss may feel, there are many others walking this path too. If you recognize something of yourself in these pages, then let that recognition remind you that you are not alone. Others, too, have stood in this silence, carried these questions, and searched for a way to keep living.

It also matters to say clearly that suicide loss should not remain surrounded by silence. It should not remain a taboo subject. The pain itself is already heavy enough; when silence is added to it, the isolation often grows deeper. Speaking about this kind of loss openly, carefully, and honestly cannot undo what has happened, but it can help create understanding where there has been uncertainty, and connection where there has been loneliness.

At the same time, it is important to say clearly that this book is not a form of medical or therapeutic treatment, nor can it replace one.

If, while reading, you notice that certain thoughts or memories are becoming overwhelming, that your emotional state is worsening, or that you are in acute psychological distress, it is important to seek support.

Professional help from physicians, licensed therapists, counselors, crisis services, or specialized support organizations can be an important and valuable source of care in such moments. Reaching for support is not a weakness. For many people, it is a necessary and deeply important step.

It can also be relieving to speak with others about what has been lived through. Many bereaved people find comfort in conversations with those who have faced something similar, or with people who are willing to listen without rushing in with explanations, advice, or ready-made answers. Sometimes it is precisely in those conversations that a sense of being understood becomes possible again.

If this book offers anything, let it be this: a small measure of recognition, a little more language for what may have felt unspeakable, and the reminder that even in grief, silence does not have to be the final answer.

About The Author

Romina Ericksen is the founder of Herzwärts - Leben nach dem Suizid® , a platform and support space created for people whose lives have been profoundly changed by suicide loss.

Her work grows out of personal experience. She knows from her own life how deeply the suicide of a loved one can alter not only the structure of everyday life, but also the way a person sees relationships, grief, memory, and the questions that remain afterward. Out of that experience came the desire to create a space in which those living with a similar loss would not have to remain alone with their thoughts, their emotions, and the often overwhelming contradictions that can follow such a rupture.

Through Herzwärts - Leben nach dem Suizid® , Romina Ericksen supports people in the German-speaking world whose lives have been fundamentally changed by suicide. Her work is for bereaved individuals who are trying to find their own way through grief, unanswered questions, emotional disorientation, and the often conflicting inner realities that can emerge after such a loss.

At the center of her work is the conviction that each person must be allowed their own path through grief. There are no fixed rules for what such a path should look like, no single timetable, and no universally correct way of carrying what has happened. Some people long for conversation and connection with others who understand. Others need first to find language for their own inner world, or simply a protected space in which their thoughts can begin to settle. Herzwärts offers that kind of space: one shaped by reflection, honest conversation, and personal accompaniment, always with respect for the individual story each person carries.

In her work, Romina Ericksen brings together personal experience and an open, direct, and compassionate approach to a subject that is still far too often surrounded by silence. One of her central concerns is to create greater understanding and to make visible that people bereaved by suicide do not have to remain alone with their questions, their memories, or their grief.

Herzwärts is for those who are looking for orientation, who want help making sense of what they are carrying, or who long for a space in which grief, remembrance, and the reality of continuing to live can be spoken about without pressure, without fixed expectations, and without having to fit into someone else's idea of how healing should look.

Alongside her support work, Romina Ericksen is committed to drawing greater attention to the reality of life after suicide loss. She speaks publicly about the experiences of those left behind and about the importance of addressing this subject more openly, more honestly, and with greater human understanding. At the heart of her work is the belief that even after a loss that changes everything, there can still be a way forward, not by erasing what happened, but by learning, slowly and in one's own time, how to keep living with one's story.

Her own path stands as part of that hope: that life after such a rupture is not the end of meaning, connection, or movement, and that continuing to live is possible, even when it once seemed unimaginable.

More information about her work and support offerings can be found at: www.herzwaerts-nach-suizid.de

For My Children

If you ever read these words one day, there is something I want you to know with absolute clarity: whether or not it was always spoken aloud, and even though life has changed around us in ways none of us would ever have chosen for ourselves, I am endlessly proud of you.

Not only because of what you have done or what you may one day do, but even more because of the things that are not always visible from the outside.

I am proud of your strength in moments when there were no easy answers, of the way you kept going even when life became heavy, of the way your hearts remained open even after pain entered your story, and of the quiet courage with which you have carried things that would have shaken many people far more than they might ever admit.

You have lived through things no child should ever have to live through, and I know that such experiences leave traces, even when those traces cannot always be seen.

That is why I want to tell you, with all the honesty and love I have, how deeply sorry I am that your path became so difficult at that point and that you were confronted so early with something that never should have belonged to your lives.

And yet, even in the midst of that, I see you.

I see the way you are growing into yourselves. I see the way you are finding your own place in the world, step by step and in your own time. I see the way each of you is becoming who you are in ways that are entirely your own. And I know that you will continue to find your way, not perfectly, not without doubt, not without days that feel hard or uncertain, but with enough strength, enough depth, and enough life in you to claim your own place in this world.

Wherever life takes you, whatever choices you make, and however your path unfolds, there is one thing I hope you will never doubt:

I am here. Always. And I love you with all my heart. Not only in the easy seasons. Not only in the moments when life feels light and everything seems to fall into place. I love you also in the difficult times, in the moments when you doubt yourselves, when you feel lost, when you do not know what to do next, or when the world feels heavier than it should. My love for you does not depend on whether you are strong, certain, successful, or okay. It is there in all of it.

You do not have to walk through life alone, even if there may be moments when it feels that way.

You are not alone.

And you never were.

Copyright and Publication Information

Bibliographic information published by the German National Library:

The German National Library lists this publication in the German National Bibliography; detailed bibliographic data are available online at dnb.dnb.de.

Herzwärts – Leben nach dem Suizid®

Publisher:

BoD · Books on Demand GmbH

Überseering 33

22297 Hamburg

bod@bod.de

Printing:

Libri Plureos GmbH

Friedensallee 273

22763 Hamburg

ISBN: 978-3-6957-2483-3